Strolling Through
Milwaukee's Ethnic History

Jill Florence Lackey and Rick Petrie

MECAH Publishing

Milwaukee Ethnic Collection of Arts and Humanities

Milwaukee, Wisconsin   *http://mecahmilwaukee.com/*

For more information on this book, or to order, visit http://mecahmilwaukee.com/

ISBN-13: 978-1530039159

ISBN-10: 1530039150

Table of Contents

Cover photo by George Baker and Rick Petrie. Backdrop photo: artist unknown, cropped from https://en.wikipedia.org/wiki/Portal:United_States/Selected_panorama. Inside photos by Rick Petrie unless otherwise indicated.

Introduction

Between 2000 and 2012 Urban Anthropology Inc. conducted a study of ethnicity in Milwaukee County. Over 400 interviews of people in more than 60 ethnic groups were conducted. The study resulted in the book, *American Ethnicity in the Twenty-first Century: The Milwaukee Study* by Dr. Jill Florence Lackey (Lexington books, 2013). This book is currently used in college classrooms. The staff at Urban Anthropology Inc. wanted to produce a book designed for a local lay audience, hence the current publication was planned.

Strolling through Milwaukee's Ethnic History provides an "up close and personal" look at local ethnic life by directing readers to the neighborhoods and venues where the groups left their marks. It brings readers directly into their experiences, whether it involves strolling through the environments they built or participating in contemporary ethnic activities.

There are surely other venues in Milwaukee where ethnic activity can be seen. The best place in Milwaukee to experience multiculturalism at one venue is at the Holiday Folk Fair International held annually in November (see http://www.folkfair.org/location.html). Other sites include the great exhibits at the Milwaukee Public Museum (see https://www.mpm.edu/) and various ethnic festivals at the Henry J. Maier Festival Park (see http://milwaukeeworldfestival.com/calendar-of-events).

Outline of book

Strolling through Milwaukee's Ethnic History provides historic journeys into the experiences of some of the main ethnic groups in Milwaukee County. Chapter One includes historical walking tours of Milwaukee County ethnic groups with populations of at least 25,000 in Milwaukee County in 2010. These include (in alphabetical order) African Americans, Germans, Irish, Italians, Mexicans, and Poles. The narrative invites readers to learn the history and local contributions of these groups by walking the paths they took during significant periods of their history. Each segment ends with a short description of current ethnic activity that might interest readers.

Chapter Two includes information on those ethnic groups that had populations of more than 10,000 but less than 25,000 in Milwaukee County in 2010. These include (in alphabetical order) the English, French, Hmong, Jews, and Norwegians. Each segment describes historical experiences and provides a description of some current activity that represents the group well and might interest readers.

Chapter Three includes information on special ethnic groups with populations in Milwaukee County under 10,000. By "special" the authors mean that the groups (a) made significant contributions to the history of Milwaukee County, (b) are currently on the rise in the area, or (c) had engaging experiences in Milwaukee County. These include (in alphabetical order) the Burmese, Czechs/Slovaks, Greeks, Kashubes, North American Indians, Puerto Ricans, and Scots.

Acknowledgements

The authors wish to thank Dr. Alice Kehoe for her assistance in copy editing, and the many leaders of ethnic communities for assisting us in reviewing the chapters. The authors would also like to thank Bob Greene for sharing information on the Merrill Park neighborhood.

Chapter One: Major populations

Chapter One covers the ethnic groups that had populations of at least 25,000 in Milwaukee County in 2010. They are the African Americans, Germans, Irish, Italians, Mexicans, and Poles. The groups will be presented historically, per the time of arrival of large population waves.

While each of the ethnic groups presented had multiple areas they settled in Milwaukee County, this book focuses on the areas where the groups tended to have the most influence. Put on your most comfortable shoes, dress for the weather, and enjoy your strolls through Milwaukee ethnic history!

Milwaukee's City Hall, by German architect, Henry H. Koch

The Germans

To understand Milwaukee at all is to know something about the German presence here. The Germans began arriving in large numbers in the 1840s before Milwaukee was even a city. When Solomon Juneau became Milwaukee's first mayor in 1846, the inaugural address was printed in both English and German. As today, the Germans were remarkably diverse in cultural practices, social class, and religion.

Within a few years of their arrival, German development could be seen everywhere in Milwaukee. Most of the city's north side was settled by Germans and in time the city became known worldwide as the "German Athens." Let's take a walk through that era.

A literal walk through Milwaukee's German history

Let's begin at the Pfister Hotel on the corner of Jefferson Street and Wisconsin Avenue. Once you've arrived, you'll note the beauty of the Romanesque Revival building. It was built in 1893 by Guido Pfister, a German immigrant who also owned a tanning business.

Next, walk west two blocks to Broadway, turn right, and continue on for three more blocks. There you will find Old St. Mary's Church. The church was built in 1846 and was the central home of German Catholic immigrants. Read the inscriptions.

You are at the corner of Kilbourn Avenue and Broadway. Walk north and you will be on the campus of the Milwaukee School of Engineering. The college was built in 1903 by the Germans who believed that Milwaukee needed a technical workforce. Stroll north through the lovely campus, taking in the view.

When you reach Highland Avenue (a pedestrian street), turn west and continue to 270 East Highland Avenue. Here you will find the Blatz Building. Today it houses condos but it was originally opened as the City Brewery in 1846 by Johann Braun and became the Valentin Blatz Brewery in 1889. It was one of the top German breweries in the city. A jingle well-known across the country in the middle of the twentieth century was "I'm from Milwaukee, and I ought to know; It's draft-brewed Blatz beer wherever you go."

Feeling a little of the German presence now? There's much more. On Highland Avenue, walk three blocks to North

Water Street and turn south. Continue on for several blocks to Wells Street. You will pass the majestic City Hall, designed by Henry C. Koch in the Flemish Renaissance Revival style and completed in 1895. Turn west on Wells. There you will run into the gorgeous Pabst Theater. It was commissioned in 1895 by Frederick Pabst, another beer baron and designed by architect Otto Strack to resemble the European opera houses, again in the Renaissance Revival style. It clearly represented the best in the German Athens tradition.

Next, walk west on Wells Street over the bridge and just past Plankinton Avenue to the eight-story Germania building. It was built in 1896 with the statue of Germania on a plinth over the door as the symbol of Germany. The building was home to a number of German publications. The name was changed to the Brumder Building in 1918 in response to anti-German sentiments in Milwaukee following World War One.

Now continue about two blocks west on Wells Street until you reach Old World Third Street. Turn north and walk three blocks. You will notice Usinger's Sausage, a major German enterprise in Milwaukee.

Check out the rest of the block. You will also notice the very ornate Mader's restaurant. Stop here to look inside and glance at the menu. Have you ever tried dishes named *Rheinischer Sauerbraten*, *Wiener Schinitzel*, *Kasseler Rippchen*, *Rouladen*, or *Ritter Schnitzel*?

Your final stop is Turner Hall, which is just around the corner on North Fourth Street between State Street and Highland Avenue. Constructed in 1882 by the same German architect who designed City Hall and the Pfister Hotel—Henry H. Koch—Turner Hall became home to the Milwaukee Turners.

The first Turner Societies in the United States were founded by German immigrants and exiles who left Europe during the failed revolutions of 1848. The refugees subsequently became known as the Forty Eighters.

Go inside Turner Hall and look around. Note the gymnasium. The Turner societies, following their German models, were mainly gymnastic clubs that also promoted the right of free speech and clean government. Many of the Forty Eighters and Turner members would become active in liberal movements nationwide and even worldwide, such as the Socialists. The Socialist movement in Milwaukee began in the 1850s. The movement increased in momentum until it reached its peak among workers in the early twentieth century. During the century, three elected mayors and one congressman in Milwaukee were Socialists, as were scores of other political office holders across the county.

Next, walk through the restaurant/beer hall on the first floor of Turner Hall. Look at the photographs and the wall plaques. Note the emphasis on a fully-lived life. The success of Socialism in Milwaukee had much to do with German practices here. According to German scholar, Don Heinrich Tolzman, in the *German American Experience*, Germans brought with them "a large capacity for the enjoyment of life." Among the leisure time activities that Germans contributed in mass to US culture were music, theater, art, architecture, gymnastics, and a penchant for Sunday frolicking.

Now walk upstairs to the Turner Hall ballroom. Stroll about and experience more of the German fully-lived life. During the height of the Socialist influence locally, most of the voting population in Milwaukee also shared German roots and probably recognized cultural affinities with the Socialists—most of whom were Germans themselves. The Socialists were the only political party locally to oppose Prohibition early in the twentieth century, an issue that clearly united Germans in Milwaukee. In addition, Socialist community events such as bazaars, minstrel shows, plays, and picnics were well attended by members of the greater Milwaukee community.

It is time to stop and eat a little German food. Enjoy something at Turner Hall or return to Mader's on Old World Third. Do you now have a better understanding of the Germans in the history of Milwaukee?

But what about the Germans today?

"The Germans have a history of being involved in healthy activities, with the nature walks and the gymnastics."

"My grandfather was always so proud of the fact that by the time that he came to America to the time he retired, he never missed a day of work. There was never a day he didn't work. That was typical in the German community. Nobody wanted to miss a day of work."

Quotes of German informants from the 12-year ethnic study conducted by Urban Anthropology Inc.

Milwaukee Germans today

World Wars One and Two took their toll on the German influence in Milwaukee. Fearing the post-war backlash, large numbers of Germans changed their names. Schmidts became Smiths; Brauns became Browns; Muellers became Millers. The German press nearly disappeared. Many ethnic Germans moved from the City of Milwaukee into the suburbs.

But not all German culture disappeared in Milwaukee County. In addition to German Fest held each summer on Milwaukee's lakefront, Oktoberfests are celebrated everywhere. One of the best places to participate in this festival is at the fabulous Old Heidelberg Park at 700 West Lexington Boulevard, Glendale.

Prost!

The Irish

While some Irish had been in the United States prior to the American Revolution, a large wave of Irish immigrants arrived during and shortly after the Irish Potato Famine of 1845 to 1852. Many of those who came to Milwaukee took jobs in the Third Ward. At the time of their arrival the Ward was mostly swamp land with some Yankee and German commercial buildings located on the Lake Michigan coast. The merchants needed the swamp cleared and infrastructure built. With one wagon full of dirt at a time, the Irish filled in the area and constructed roads. They built cottages between the Milwaukee River and the lake—cottages so small and so close together that residents could literally stretch out their hands from their windows and touch the houses next door

Many of the Irish had family members who settled in Chicago and the Third Ward Irish would take steamers down Lake Michigan to visit their relatives. Then tragedy struck. In 1860 the steamship *The Lady Elgin* sank off the coast of Chicago on the return trip and 300 Irish died. This was the second greatest shipwreck ever on the Great Lakes.

But this was not the end of the Irish tragedies in the Third Ward. In 1892 the Ward burned to the ground. It was Milwaukee's worst fire

ever, and had a lot to do with congested streets and alleyways. Commerce was so consolidated in the Ward that by 1890 the businesses, industries and railroad yards were stacking their lumber, coal, and oil drums wherever there was room. The Irish fire chief of the time, James Foley, made the argument that firefighting equipment could not pass blocked back-roads, alleys, and entrances to docks to fight any fires that might occur.

Representation of Captain Foley in the Third Ward

Foley brought this issue to the Common Council but nothing was done to relieve the congested areas. Foley then argued in support of a fire boat to fight potential fires from the river shores. The fireboat *Cataract* was built and was stationed in the Milwaukee River. All of this played roles in the Third Ward Fire of 1892.

Virtually all the homes were destroyed in this fire. The Irish had to move on. Fortunately, some of the Irish found a new neighborhood in a newly developing project on Milwaukee's west side—Merrill Park.

A literal walk through Milwaukee's Irish history

While nothing but markers exist to acknowledge the Irish presence in the Third Ward, this is surely not the case in Merrill Park. Here you will see much of the built environment of the four P's of Irish life—parish, pub, politics, and performance. We will begin our walk at the corner of North Thirtieth Street and Michigan.

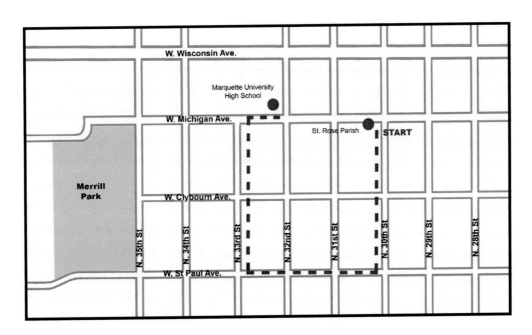

You are on the block of St. Rose *Parish* (the first P of Irish life). (The Irish called this church "St. Rose's.") In its heyday—between the 1930s and 1960s—the parish had seven Sunday services at 5:30, 6:30, 7:30, 9:00, 10:00, 11:00, and noon. The last four services were often standing room only. But St. Rose's wasn't just a place to worship. It was also the community center for the Merrill Park Irish. The doors of St. Rose were open 24 hours a day, and activities ranged from Catholic rites, to social clubs, to classes on living skills, to family counseling, to youth recreation, to neighborhood planning.

Let's walk south on Thirtieth Street. Here we will pass the St. Rose school, which is today consolidated as the St. Rose and St. Leo Catholic School. The original school was founded in 1893. As you walk, look on the east side of the street. This area was once lined with *pubs* (another P of Irish life). The developer of Merrill Park, Sherburn S. Merrill, banned taverns in his development (with a western boundary that ended on the east side of Thirtieth Street), hence the Irish inhabitants and others built pubs just across the street. The same was true on the eastern border of Merrill's development, at North Twenty-Seventh Street.

If *parish* life was the model for community ideals among the Merrill Park Irish, *pub* life was the guide to social relationships. Pub life was an import from rural Ireland, with a few new twists. In Ireland, English limits on industrialization and restrictions on the kinds of crops Irish farmers could raise helped create a society in which marriage of the offspring was delayed to provide manual labor for the farm, and support for the parents. Without spouses and children of their own, young people had little to do after dark. Many found the local pub a place to relieve loneliness.

But in America, marriages were not necessarily delayed. The pub remained a strong focal point for socializing among many urban Irish, but only occasionally after dark. In Merrill Park, the pubs were often stopping-off points for men and women on their way home from work.

In a moment we will turn west on West Clybourn Street and enter the area called "political row," but first, we'll continue south to St. Paul Avenue and get a glimpse of Merrill Park's past *performance* life (another P of Irish life). Look across the street. See the lot with all the crops growing? That was once the site of the Irish Village Pub where drinking and story-telling were the activities of the night.

But there's a performance site even more compelling on this block. On the corner of St. Paul Avenue and Thirtieth Street (3001 West St. Paul Avenue), there is a house that once belonged to the Irish Tracy family. Young Spencer Tracy grew up there. He was an altar boy at St. Rose's before moving on into a phenomenal career in acting, including two Academy Awards and nine nominations.

Let's return to Clybourn Street and move west. You may notice that the homes in Merrill Park are very large and often ornate. While the Irish coming from the Third Ward were generally poor and many took entry level jobs at the railroad yards just a few blocks south of where you now stand, many also worked their way up the economic ladder—often through jobs and offices in the public sector. We are now in the area known as political row. *Politics* (another P of Irish life) was a very successful activity in Merrill Park. In fact, when researchers from Urban Anthropology Inc. conducted an oral history of the neighborhood they learned that in one half century alone in the 1900s, Merrill Park produced nearly 100 judges, district attorneys, and state, county, and city legislators and municipal department heads. During this period, three of four county executives were Merrill Parkers. And three of four Milwaukee mayors were raised in the neighborhood.

The area labeled "political row" extends to North Thirty-Third Street. While not even half of the residents of Merrill Park were Irish, the Irish influence was everywhere. Even some non-Irish took an interest in politics. Turn north on Thirty-Third Street and stop at 504 North Thirty-Third Street. This was the childhood home of Carl and Frank Zeidler, two past mayors of Milwaukee.

Continue walking to Michigan and turn east. You will pass Marquette High School, which was founded in 1925. Many of the Irish young people graduated from this school. As you are heading east on your way back to the starting point of the tour, turn right on Thirty-Second Street on the east side of the street and stop at 546 North Thirty-Second Street. This is the home of William O'Donnell, a former Milwaukee County Executive who served in that office from 1977 to 1988. He lived in this house most of his life and did not have a driver's license until his sixties. He took the bus everywhere and even took neighborhood kids to the lakefront by bus in his younger days.

Now return to your starting point. On the way you might wonder why so few Irish live in Merrill Park today. One reason was I 94. The building of this freeway removed about one-third of the Merrill Park neighborhood, making it necessary for many Irish (and others) to seek housing in other communities. Another reason for the exodus was the consolidation of many hospitals under the county direction of Executive John Doyne in the late 1970s. Many Irish had been employed at hospitals just blocks from Merrill Park, including Doctor's, Children's Samaritan, and Deaconess Hospitals. When these were consolidated at the County Grounds in Wauwatosa, many Irish followed their jobs and moved to that suburb.

"Irish stories can go on for days. We have this event close to Halloween, called *Samhain*, where we all go out to the woods, gather around a campfire, and listen to Irish stories, some of them very mystical."

"The unions were very powerful and we hung out in certain bars. We used to decide everything in the bar — who would get this job and that job, who would run for this or that office, how we would get people jobs at the county."

Quotes of Irish informants from the 12-year ethnic study conducted by Urban Anthropology Inc.

Milwaukee Irish today

Surprisingly, the moves out of Merrill Park did not end cultural life for the urban Irish. The parishes and pubs still brought the community back. Merrill Parkers continue to gather at least once a month at St. Rose Parish or in Irish pubs to talk about old times, and political life is still the talk of the day.

The Irish also gather at the Irish Cultural and Heritage Center at 2133 West Wisconsin Avenue or at Irish Fest on the Summerfest grounds in August. But the main venue to experience everything Irish is at the annual St. Patrick's Day Parade in March of every year, usually held on Plankinton Avenue and Old World Third Street between Wisconsin and Juneau Avenues. Here you will see marching bands, pipers, Irish dancers, floats, and Irish celebrities. There are parties throughout the day and night with food, entertainment, and beverages. To learn the exact date and location, go to http://saintpatricksparade.org/.

The Poles

Polish immigrants began arriving in the United States in large numbers after the Civil War. Much of Milwaukee's south side was developed by Poles. The Poles were less diverse than the Germans. Like the Irish, nearly all were Catholic.

A literal walk through Milwaukee's Polish history

To feel the influence of the Poles in Milwaukee, let's begin at South Sixth Street and Lincoln Avenue. There you'll be overwhelmed by the majestic presence of the Basilica of St. Josaphat. Look up. Try and visualize Polish men and women on scaffolding in 1899, building this edifice with their own hands.

Let's go inside. Enter the Basilica at the Pope John Paul II Pavilion on Lincoln Avenue near South Seventh Street. Visitors are welcome on weekdays between 10am and 4pm (and of course for services at other times). Walk through the pavilion and note all the stained glass windows donated over the years by Milwaukee Poles.

Be prepared to lose your breath as you enter the sanctuary. This basilica is as beautiful as any you will find in Rome or Florence. Walk around. Look up. Note the sacred texts written in Polish.

Next, go down to the lower level. There you will find the lower sanctuary, which is also an extraordinary work of art. On the same level you'll see an exhibit of photos and diagrams that tell the full story of how the basilica was originally built and later restored.

When you exit the basilica, cross Lincoln Avenue. On the north side of the street is the Little Friar's Shop where you can window shop for Catholic and Polish gifts.

Next, continue west on Lincoln. As you cross Seventh Street you will be at the entrance to Kosciuszko Park, named after the famous Polish Revolutionary War hero, General Thaddeus Kosciuszko. This park was once the center of Polish public life on Milwaukee's south side. Today it is still used for Polish processions on holidays such as Polish Constitution Day in early May.

Before you continue west, look across the street. There you will see the lovely Old South Side Settlement Museum. The museum tells the story of the history of the neighborhood with recreated rooms of the major ethnic groups that settled the area. On the front of the museum is a plaque telling you how you can reserve a tour to the museum. The tours last about one-half hour and are most enlightening about the families that lived in this neighborhood.

Continue walking west for several blocks until you arrive at Kosciuszko Monument Square. Here you will see the newly restored statue of the General. In 1905, over 60,000 Poles attended the original dedication of the monument. Read the inscriptions, and then sit for a moment and enjoy the view.

After your stop, continue west on West Lincoln Avenue. Note the interesting architectural styles of the commercial buildings. Atop their roofs you will see curly and angular parapets. This style was brought to Milwaukee by the Poles of northern Poland.

When you reach South Eleventh Street, cross the street and walk one block south. There you will encounter the Holy Name of Jesus Church. This is a Polish National Catholic Church that keeps most Catholic traditions but is governed by its own synod. This church was consecrated by the south side Poles in 1917 and is still attended by many local Polish Americans.

Getting a little hungry? You can finish your tour of Polish history by returning to Lincoln Avenue and walking one block west. There you will find the A&J Polish Deli. This is perhaps the last commercial establishment in Milwaukee where you will find most signage in the Polish language. Enjoy a lunch or a snack!

"There was the election of the Pope and the Solidarity movement in Poland, and that gave a big boost to our community. The [*Leonardo da Vinci and the*] *Art of Poland* art exhibit here was big. People can say, 'We really are important.' The Polish here have had an inferiority complex. It's important to have the outside world notice, like with Walensa and [the] Nobel Peace Prize."

"The Catholic Church is involved in all parts of our lives. It's life centered on the parish. We had sixteen to eighteen Polish parishes then in the city, and still have several.

Quotes of Polish informants from the 12-year ethnic study conducted by
Urban Anthropology Inc.

Milwaukee Poles today

While about 20 percent of the residents that live along the path you have just traveled are still Polish, most of the Poles began moving out of the neighborhood in the 1960s when the freeway took much of the eastern section of the neighborhood, creating housing shortages. Many moved into the southern suburbs.

Today, the best place to experience Polish culture in Milwaukee County is at the Polish Center of Wisconsin in Franklin (6941 South Sixty-Eighth Street). This extraordinary building was built in the style of a Polish manor house and overlooks a beautiful spring-fed lake in a natural wooded setting.

Polish events at this center are diverse and well-attended. They include concerts, bingo games, weddings, beer and vodka tasting events, special art exhibits, a pierogi festival, workshops, classes, and dedications. For specific descriptions and times of events, check out the center's website at http://polishcenterofwisconsin.org/.

The Italians

Italian immigrants began arriving in large waves to the United States in the 1880s. In Milwaukee, a significant number of Sicilians ended up in the downtown area in the early 1890s. This was due to the Third Ward fire of 1892 that had leveled practically every building and scattered the Irish population that had settled the area earlier. The Sicilian immigrants were invited to join a labor force to rebuild the Ward and work in its shipping industry. Many of these Sicilians were from Porticello, a fishing village on the island's north coast.

The Third Ward remained mostly Italian until the 1960s, when, like so many ethnic neighborhoods you are visiting, it was raised by urban renewal and freeway building.

Let us look for remnants of this community.

A literal walk through Milwaukee's Italian history

To feel the influence of the Italians in Milwaukee, we will begin at the River Walk at Buffalo and North Water Streets in the Third Ward. It was here and along the shores of Lake Michigan that the fire boat the *Cataract* fought the blaze that would ultimately destroy the Third Ward and send its Irish population into other areas, such as Merrill Park. It was on these waterways and at these ports that the Italians arrived in Milwaukee.

Look around at the beautiful buildings you see. Many of these had originally been warehouses. The Italians rebuilt this entire area between 1895 and 1940. During that time period the Ward became known as "Little Italy."

33

The local Italians, like Milwaukee's Irish and Poles, were almost all Catholic. They tended to express their faith in street festivals and religious processions. The early arriving Sicilians built a church of their own, the Blessed Virgin of Pompei, on Jackson Street, which was nicknamed the "little pink church." We will see the site of that church in a minute.

Let's walk along North Water Street north to St. Paul Avenue and continue east to Broadway. On the way, we'll pass Milwaukee's Public Market.

The inspiration for this establishment was Little Italy's Commission Row. From the start, the Italians were very entrepreneurial and found their niche in the food industry. By 1920 the Italian Ward had 45 grocers and 2 spaghetti factories. They founded Milwaukee's first pizza restaurant, the Caradara Club, in the Third Ward right after World War Two and later opened Italian restaurants all over the city. But one of their more interesting ventures was the open-air market they developed at the turn of the twentieth century. Begin walking south on Broadway toward Buffalo Street. This was the area called Commission Row. Here fruit and vegetable wholesalers peddled their wares at the curbside to Milwaukee-area grocers and restaurants. It earned its name because the salesmen used to work strictly on commission.

Commission Row stayed active until early in the twenty-first century. Many of the vendors left early, as supermarkets out-competed corner grocers and pushcart industries. But this block of Broadway, between St. Paul Avenue and Buffalo Street, hosted three large wholesalers. When Jennaro Brothers, the final wholesaler, closed down, the Historic Third Ward Association committed to return some semblance of these public markets and the Italian presence to the Ward. And this is what you just passed—the Public Market.

Other ways that this neighborhood has tried to bring back the Italian presence is through Festa Italiana at the Third Ward Summerfest Grounds on the lakefront and the opening of the striking Italian Community Center which we will see next.

Once you've reached Buffalo Street at Broadway, walk one block south to Chicago Street and head three and one-half blocks east. There you will have the opportunity to visit the Italian Community and Conference Center. Walk around the grounds and inside. Look at the photos on the walls. This will give you the best possible feel for the daily life of "Little Italy." Note the "little pink church," the processions, street vendors, weddings, and rich family life.

If you are feeling hungry, stop at La Scala inside the community center and enjoy authentic Italian cuisine. Or sit outside in the courtyard and enjoy Italian music on select summer nights.

On your return trip you might want to stop and visit the historic marker for the Blessed Virgin of Pompeii church. It can be found under the freeway ramp at the intersection of Jackson and Van Buren Streets.

Milwaukee Italians today

One of the best places to experience Italian life today is at the annual Festa Italiana mass and procession that takes place each July. The mass is held Sunday at the Marcus Ampitheater usually at 11 am and is followed by a procession of floats of Italian societies and patron saints. It is concluded with a benediction at the Summerfest Festival Grounds.

The "pink church" is impressively represented on procession floats, as are other markers of Italian life back to Italy and through the presence in the Third Ward. The Marcus Ampitheater is located on the Summerfest grounds.

For specific annual dates, check out the Festa Italiana website at http://festaitaliana.com/.

The African Americans

African Americans were in Milwaukee from the time of Solomon Juneau, whose cook was black. Early in Milwaukee's history, the population was scattered in small numbers all over the city. This changed during the time of the Great Migration (1910-1930) when African Americans migrated from the South to northern cities in greater numbers. It was during those years that African Americans began joining Germans, Jews, and others on Milwaukee's near north side.

The area *roughly* between Martin Luther King Drive (then North Third) and North Twelfth Streets and between Juneau and North Avenues became known as Bronzeville—an

African American community. Walnut Street was the main business and entertainment center. However, in the 1950s and 1960s two government programs displaced this community. One program was the Urban Renewal Administration, which had been designed to improve central city housing. Many blocks in Bronzeville were slated for revitalization, and residents on these blocks were forced to sell over 8,000 homes. During the same time period, the Milwaukee County Expressway Commission was building two major freeway corridors in the heart of the City. One cut directly across Bronzeville, discarding Walnut Street as the center of the community.

While the original Bronzeville was nearly entirely razed, a few remnants of this community have been recreated.

A literal walk through Milwaukee's African American history

Our walk begins at the Lapham Park Apartments and Senior Center at 1901 North Sixth Street. You will be visiting a re-creation of Walnut Street as it existed in the 1940s and 1950s. (It is best to call ahead at 414-286-8859 to ensure access.) The senior citizens of Lapham Park, working with the center's management, helped to replicate several sections of Old Walnut Street from memories and photos and some actual belongings of the residents.

Once inside, walk around. Check out the shops. Read the inscriptions. Note the photos of old Bronzeville on the walls. Try and imagine this self-contained black community in its heyday with nearly 500 businesses that thrived on this ground.

When you leave the Lapham Park Center, you will cross North Sixth Street and walk east. You are in the lovely Halyard Park Neighborhood that extends from Martin Luther King Drive on the east to North Sixth Street on the west, and North Avenue on the north to McKinley Avenue on the south.

When Bronzeville was completely leveled in the 1960s, a black real estate developer named Beechie Brooks began plans for this neighborhood. He saw that the City of Milwaukee had erected some housing for low income African Americans to replace the homes they'd lost, but saw little in development for middle class blacks. Brooks began a campaign to raise capital to build a new neighborhood. By the late 1970s he'd raised enough money to build Halyard Park with housing and landscapes that were state of the art for its time.

44

Walk around Halyard Park. Note the layout and quality of the homes. Stop at the Gaines Triangle on Halyard Avenue and read the inscription.

After you have finished your stroll through Halyard Park, walk north to West North Avenue. Look around. This is becoming the "new" Bronzeville. A number of African American activists have partnered with the City of Milwaukee to create a new commercial and entertainment district that will attempt to mirror the area's past. Some installments are already in place. Note the new Urban League headquarters at 435 West North Avenue. Note the newly rehabbed Inner City Arts Council building—renovated by the Vangard Group.

The boundaries of the new Bronzeville District are Martin Luther King Drive to North Seventh Street and Garfield Avenue to Center Street (with some developments possibly extending as far north as Chambers Street and as far south as Lloyd Street).

> "Jazz and blues are from memory and is still like this. With Europeans it's different—succinctly—they will play the same song twice exactly the same. This won't be the case with African Americans. It's how we see the world."
>
> "The loss of Bronzeville was the breakdown of the village. The whites had people moving them into the projects and those with a little money moved to the suburbs. It was then the image of who we were that came from the whites. Before that it had been a localized culture. Before that you took care of your own—you watched other people's kids, made sure your neighborhood was nice and safe. After the move, we lost that."
>
> *Quotes of African Americans from the 12-year ethnic study conducted by Urban Anthropology Inc.*

Milwaukee African Americans today

While the new Bronzeville District is a work in progress, you might ask where one might go to enjoy an authentic African American experience today. The answer is the annual Juneteenth Day celebration.

Juneteenth Day, observed on June 19th, is the US holiday that commemorates the day in 1865 when the end of slavery was announced in Texas. In Milwaukee, the holiday is celebrated all day along Martin Luther King Drive between Center and Burleigh Streets. It is a street festival with everything African American—the food, families, music, clothes, dance, exhibits, crafts, art, and a parade. Various demonstrations of art, culinary skills, drumming, and rapping roll out spontaneously or in staged areas. The streets are literally packed with people all day long.

The Mexicans

The first significant wave of Mexicans arrived in Milwaukee in 1922. The Pfister-Vogel Tannery on South Sixth Street recruited 100 Mexican men to take the jobs of striking Anglos. The Mexicans, who were recruited from the town of Tangancicuaro, Michuacan, did not initially know that they were given work contracts to break a strike. They settled in barracks set up by the tannery and later looked for available housing in nearby neighborhoods. These recruits, and some who took railroad and other jobs, became known as *los primeros*.

The early population settled mostly in the Walker's Point neighborhood where they founded Mexican businesses and self-help organizations. Because most of the *primeros* were men, they often married Polish women whose families were already settled on Milwaukee's south side.

A literal walk through Milwaukee's Mexican history

Our walk begins at the United Community Center (UCC) at 1028 South Ninth Street in the Walker's Square section of the Walker's Point neighborhood. The UCC is a comprehensive, sociocultural organization that serves all populations on Milwaukee's south side and offers a rich array of Latino cultural programs. Unfortunately, little remains of the original Mexican neighborhood in Walker's Point. Many of the buildings have been torn down and entire blocks were lost when the freeway I-94 was constructed in the area. Fortunately, the UCC was able to retain some of the Mexican cultural history in exhibits and murals.

Go inside. Immediately you will notice the wealth of historic photos on the walls. Walk through the halls and read the captions. Many of Milwaukee's leading (as well as relatively unknown) Latino families are represented in this vast historic collection.

In the main hall, you will notice two enclosed exhibits. These commemorate the economic lives of the Mexican *primeros* and their children, who took jobs in tanneries and foundries. Read the captions.

From the main hall you can access another area called Latino Arts. There you can explore visual arts and current exhibits that provide another dimension of the Milwaukee Latino experience.

After you've strolled these halls, go out the same door you came in and walk north. The building next door to the UCC general entrance is the Bruce-Guadalupe Community School. Note the Blending of Cultures mural by local artist Reynaldo Hernandez.

Move to the north wall of the school adjacent to the freeway entrance ramp. Walk along this wall and learn about the fascinating history of Latinos in Milwaukee. This valuable visual narrative, painted by artist Roberto Cisneros in 1995, tells the story of the cultural foundations of Latinos in the Americas and the specific experience of Latinos in Milwaukee.

Look at panel #1. Note the first recorded Mexican in Milwaukee, music teacher Rafael Baez, who arrived in the city in 1884. Panel #2 portrays the heroes of the Mexican Revolution.

Move to panel #3 and note the visual narrative of the first wave of Mexican arrivals who came as replacement workers during the Pfister-Vogel Tannery strike.

Panel #4 narrates the early Mexican community with its neighborhoods and churches. Of particular interest is the depiction of Frederico Herrera, an early community leader who led the development of Milwaukee mutual aid society, *Asociacion Mutualista Hispano Azteca*, and the first celebration of Mexican Independence Day in Bay View in 1930.

Panel #5 depicts the Great Depression and its impact on Milwaukee Mexicans. The number of Mexicans in Milwaukee declined from nearly 4,000 in 1929 to about 1,500 in 1934. Like other populations who lost work during these years, Milwaukee's Mexicans had to take advantage of whatever charities were available to them.

Panel #6 shows the impact of World War Two on Mexican Americans. Because of a labor shortage, the Bracero program was started to bring in over 2,600 Mexican nationals as needed contract workers to Wisconsin. Many Mexican Americans also served in the military during World War Two.

Panel #7 portrays the arrival of the first major wave of Puerto Ricans in Milwaukee. In 1951, 100 Puerto Rican laborers were recruited to work at local foundries.

Panel #8 depicts the rise in Latino social activism in Milwaukee. Note the representation of Father James Groppi, Milwaukee Civil Rights leader, with Cesar Chavez, head of the United Farm Workers. Chavez came to Milwaukee in the 1960s to organize local farm workers.

Panel #9 is about equal opportunity in education. The panel shows a demonstration that led to the Spanish Speaking Outreach Institute at the University of Wisconsin-Milwaukee in 1970. This was the same year that the United Community Center was established. At the top of the panel you can see the organization's original site at St. John the Evangelist Church.

If you are feeling a little bit hungry by now, an excellent place to enjoy Mexican food can be accessed back at the United Community Center. On the way you might visit the Lady of Guadalupe Shrine at the corner of South Ninth and West Washington Streets. The sculptor of this Mexican spiritual icon was Alejandro Romero. The shrine was bestowed to the Walker Square neighborhood by the United Community Center and is open to all area residents as a spiritual retreat.

When you return to the UCC, you can experience a variety of Mexican and Puerto Rican entrees at Café el Sol. If you happen to arrive on a Friday evening, you can enjoy the fish dinner buffet that was voted as the "best ethnic adaptation" of a local fish fry by the *Journal Sentinel* in 2003. Live Mexican entertainment is also often a cultural option on Fridays between 6:30 and 8:30 pm.

"My father could barely understand English but he worked full time and overtime as a janitor in a hotel. He bought this truck and carried loads for people as a freelancer whenever he had the chance. This money he put away for us. When I went into business he took that money out of the account and gave it to me so I could start a bakery."

"As Mexicans, we want our children to stay with us until they marry. And we don't want them to move away when they have careers. But the colleges, they make it seem like the student should just get up and move away from family if they get a chance for a good job somewhere else. This is not the Mexican way — it's not the Latino way — but the kids listen to them, and now you see our communities breaking up because the kids think their professors know more than their parents. The kids say this is the American way. But what? To have a job making a few thousand dollars more, just to lose your family and friends and your ethnicity?"

Quotes of Mexican informants from the 12-year ethnic study conducted by Urban Anthropology Inc.

Milwaukee Mexican Americans today

One of the best times to observe Mexican traditions in Milwaukee today is during the Day of the Dead (*Dia de Los Muertos*). The Day of the Dead is a Mexican holiday (October 31 through November 2) that brings the community together to remember and honor friends and family members who have died and help support them on their spiritual journeys. Small altars to the deceased loved ones are often set up in homes and even in the display areas of businesses.

The day is also a time for celebration. One of Milwaukee's best day-long celebrations is at Walker's Square Park on West Washington and South Tenth Streets that includes a parade, face painting, a walk/run event, music, food, and dancers.

For information on times and activities, check out the website at http://diadelosmuertosmilwaukee.com.

Chapter Two: Minor populations

Chapter Two covers the ethnic groups that had populations between 10,000 and 24,999 in Milwaukee County in 2010. These include (in alphabetical order) the English, French, Hmong, Jews, and Norwegians. Because few of these populations dominated specific areas within Milwaukee County, there will not be walking tours of neighborhoods. However, the chapter does point readers to places and events where the groups' ethnic practices can be observed.

The groups will be presented historically, per the time of arrival of large population waves.

The French

Beginning in the seventeenth century, people of French ancestry played major roles in Wisconsin (and Milwaukee) history. They included French, French Canadians, and Metis people. The fur trade, which began in the 1680s, was well established in Wisconsin by the eighteenth century with fur posts across the state. The majority of workers in the fur trade were people of French ancestry, even though most of the fur trade companies across the country were owned by the British following the Seven Years' War (1754-1763).

Local notables

A major fur trader in Wisconsin was Jacques Vieau, a French Canadian with ancestry in Marseille, France (his great-uncle had been Governor of Marseille). Often called the "father of Milwaukee," Vieau established a winter trading post atop a bluff overlooking the Menomonee Valley in 1795. His cabin was located in the area today known as Mitchell Park, on Milwaukee's near south side. At the time of his arrival, a large number of Potawatomi, as well as some Sauk, Menomonee, and Fox, and a few Ho-Chunk were settled in the area.

Jacques Vieau was a classic *voyageur*—a man who spent part of his time in the French colonial settlements and the rest of his time among the American Indians with whom he traded European goods for furs. The voyageurs often took American Indian wives. Vieau was married to Angelique Roy, a half Menomonee woman who also had Potawatomi connections.

Vieau had many French Canadian assistants during his tenure in Milwaukee. One was his son-in-law, a voyageur named Laurent Solomon Juneau. Juneau had married Josette Vieau in 1814, and by 1818 he'd became Vieau's clerk in Milwaukee.

While Vieau eventually made his permanent home on the west banks of the Fox River at Green Bay, Solomon Juneau was becoming convinced by friends that Milwaukee was about to become the major center of trade in Wisconsin. In the 1830s Juneau platted the village of Milwaukee and settled there. He began selling plots of land in what was becoming known as Juneautown. He built Milwaukee's first store and first inn, and in 1837 founded the *Milwaukee Sentinel.*

Juneau was elected the first mayor of Milwaukee and served from 1846 until 1847. He also became the city's first postmaster.

Place names for Vieau and Juneau include Vieau School and Vieau Park on Milwaukee's south side, and Juneau Avenue and Juneau Park on Milwaukee's north side. A monument to Juneau stands in the park (see above).

Immigrants

Many early residents of Milwaukee County were descendants of the French, French Canadian, and Metis populations who settled in the area during the fur trading boom. Over the centuries others with French connections came from Canada, France, and French-speaking African countries, often to fill jobs in education. One of the largest waves of French immigration occurred immediately after World War Two when American soldiers brought home French brides. Smaller waves of French came to the United States in the late twentieth century to take professional positions at General Electric Healthcare in Brookfield and Johnson Controls in the City of Milwaukee.

To most French immigrants, maintaining food practices and keeping the language were very important. They got together with other immigrants to keep up their French language skills and enjoy French cuisine and leisurely meals. Many also made sure they returned periodically to their homeland.

"When you go back in your own country, it's more quiet; it's more cool, more calm. We have one quality of life in France. We think vacation. We stay two or three hours at the meal-table to eat and drink and laugh and recount a story. Here you don't have this. I have friends with kids, and the kids eat in the kitchen, they take their plate, and they leave. In my family, everybody stayed at the table."

Quote of French informant from the 12-year ethnic study conducted by Urban Anthropology Inc

---

Where to observe French culture

A major organization that unites people of French connections locally is Alliance Francaise of Milwaukee. Its mission is "to promote, share and enjoy the culture, language and friendship of the French-speaking world." Almost every day of the week the organization provides some kind of French conversation classes or gatherings.

Alliance Francaise and the French Program of the University of Wisconsin-Milwaukee also sponsor an annual French Film Festival on campus that is usually free to audiences. The event lasts over a week and offers up to twenty films. To access dates and other specifics, go to the website at http://uwm.edu/french-film-festival/.

An excellent place to experience everything French is during Milwaukee's Bastille Days, sponsored annually by the East Town Association. The free, four-day bash offers chef and wine demos, live music, an international marketplace, French and Cajun cuisine, roaming street performers, and its signature 43-foot Eiffel Tower replica offering hourly light shows. The event, held downtown in the vicinity of Cathedral Square, usually convenes in July. For exact dates and other information, see http://www.easttown.com/events/bastille-days/.

The English

Great Britain controlled the territory of Wisconsin between 1763 and 1815. However, because the British were mainly interested in the fur trade with the Ho-Chunk and Ojibwe people, few British immigrants actually settled permanently in the area. This began changing in the 1820s when some English immigrants made their homes in ethnic enclaves alongside Yankee families.

Outside of Milwaukee County, the British left behind place names such as Manchester, Exeter, and Leeds. Immigrants from Cornwall settled in the towns of Dodgeville and Mineral Point and nearby rural areas.

Immigrants

As in the case of the French immigrants, possibly the largest influx of British immigrants to the Milwaukee area came right after World War Two when many local soldiers who had married English women during the war brought them home to the US. The war brides developed an organization on Milwaukee's south side called Britannia, which no longer exists.

"We love poetry, we love drama, we love walking—lots of walking. We all grew up walking. I mean the age group that I am talking about—anybody over the 60—we all walked to school when we were kids. We all walked to the station."
Quote of English informant from the 12-year ethnic study conducted by Urban Anthropology Inc.

Where to observe British culture

Today, residents in Milwaukee County are very interested in everything British—from *Downton Abbey* to One Direction to the British royals to Shakespeare to Monty Python to James Bond to the BBC to Helen Mirren to Jane Austen. But there is very little actual English culture to be found within the county. One of the few examples is the Three Lions Pub on Milwaukee's East Side (3944 North Oakland Avenue). At Three Lions Pub, patrons can watch a cricket match on wide screen televisions, and try shepherd's pie, fish & chips, or a variety of English ales and spirits. The décor is British through and through and patrons are usually served food and drinks by bartenders or wait staff from the United Kingdom.

The Milwaukee British stay active. They play soccer, tennis, golf, and they walk everywhere. They also enjoy lawn bowling, practiced today by Brits and non-Brits at Lake Park (the Lawn Bowls Association is at 3131 East Newberry Boulevard). To learn more or attend a lawn bowling tournament, check out their website at www.MilwaukeeLawnBowls.com.

The Norwegians

By 1840 there were already two major Norwegian communities settled in Wisconsin—at Rock Prairie and Jefferson Prairie, in Rock County. Norwegian immigrants to rural areas followed a distinct settlement pattern. One family would purchase land and develop a farm in an unsettled area. When members of that family began to make a profit off the land, they would purchase contiguous lands and invite other family members or past neighbors in Norway to join them. The pattern would continue with the new immigrants. This would guarantee that the Norwegians settling in rural areas were surrounded by people who spoke the same language, shared similar values, and maintained Norwegian traditions.

While most early Norwegian immigrants were farmers, others brought additional skills with them. In the United States, many worked in ship building, the fishing industry, glass blowing, carpentry, and in quarries as stone cutters.

Norwegians in Milwaukee

The settlement pattern discussed above was not possible in urban areas such as Milwaukee. To maintain their culture there, Norwegians would settle in the same or nearby neighborhoods and establish their own church (almost always Lutheran) where Norwegian was spoken. In Milwaukee, one large settlement built up around Our Savior's Lutheran Church, founded in 1858, at South Ninth and Scott streets on

Milwaukee's near south side (today the church is located at 3022 West Wisconsin Avenue). Many residents of this neighborhood went on to become major leaders in the Norwegian ethnic community.

A distinct marker of the Nordic presence in Milwaukee is the bronze sculpture of Leif Erikson created by American sculptor Anne Whitney in 1887. It is located at the northern end of Juneau Park. On the sandstone base, the inscription reads, "Leif, the discoverer/son of Erik/who sailed from Iceland/and landed on this continent/A.D. 1000." In runic letters, it also reads, "Leif, son of Erik the Red."

Cultural preservation

In both rural and urban areas, Wisconsin Norwegians founded organizations to ensure cultural preservation. The largest of these is the Sons of Norway, with a mission "to promote, preserve, and cherish a lasting appreciation of the heritage and culture of Norway and other Nordic countries while growing soundly as a fraternal benefit society and offering maximum benefits to its members."

In Milwaukee, activities of the Sons of Norway, Fosselyngen Lodge #82, include *Syttende Mai* (Norwegian Independence Day) events, a Scandinavian Festival, Heritage Camp for youth, the *Lykkeringen* folk dancing group, public torsk and meatball suppers, family picnics, scholarships to families and members, a Christmas party, exhibits at the Holiday Folk Fair, a monthly member magazine, and newsletters. Many of these events are held at the Norway House at 7507 West Oklahoma Avenue.

Norwegians in Milwaukee still enjoy traditional foods such as *lefse, lutefisk*, and *rommegrot* . Many also engage in art forms such as rosemaling and hardanger. Rosemaling is a style of painting on wood that uses geometric patterns, stylized flower ornamentation, and **scrollwork**, often in flowing patterns. **Hardanger** is a form of **embroidery** often used on national costumes that is traditionally worked with white thread on white cloth, using **counted** thread and **drawn thread work** techniques.

Notable locals

A notable Norwegian intellectual with Milwaukee ties was Thorstein Veblen. **Thorstein Veblen was a nationally renowned early sociologist and economist. Born the son of Norwegian parents who immigrated to Milwaukee in 1847, Veblen developed theories of business and the leisure class. His family's experience getting to America was traumatic. Parents Thomas Anderson and Kari Veblen endured a four and one-half month trip on the Atlantic, where the couple and their children protracted a disease. All the children died aboard the ship and Thorstein was born later in 1857 in Cato, Wisconsin. He be-**came a leader of the **institutional economics** movement and is credited for the main technical principle used by institutional economists, known as the **Veblenian dichotomy. It is a** distinction between what Veblen called "institutions" and "technology."

Another notable was John Norquist. Born in New Jersey in 1949 of Norwegian and Swedish parents, Norquist and his family moved to Milwaukee where he became the city's 37th mayor between 1988 and 2003. He was mostly responsible for bringing design principles of the New Urbanism to Milwaukee that led to breakthrough developments downtown, in the Third Ward, and along the banks of the Milwaukee River. Norquist's father, Reverend Ernest O. Norquist, was a founding member of the local Nordic Council that worked to consolidate the interests and activities of all Nordic countries.

Where to observe Norwegian culture

One of the best places to meet and observe local Norwegians practicing their culture today is at a torsk dinner at the Norway House at 7507 West Oklahoma Avenue. The dinners once included only a traditional Norwegian entree of boiled or baked cod purchased in Maine. But today they also feature favorites from Finland and Sweden, such as meat balls, pea soup, ethnic drinks, salads, dumplings, and potato dishes. The dinners are usually held once a month from September through April and draw up to 200 people each time. This is a great chance to eat a wonderful meal while chatting with Nordic people about their experiences at long banquet tables.

To check prices and dates, go to http://www.norwayhouse-milw.org/.

The Jews

A small Jewish population lived in the Milwaukee area in the early nineteenth century. By 1850, there were 70 Jewish families in the city. By 1895, the number of families increased to over 200.

Immigrants

Early on, most of Milwaukee's Jewish population came from Germany and surrounding nations of Austria, Hungary, and Bohemia. In time, this pattern shifted and most of the Jewish immigrants began arriving from Eastern Europe. In the 1980s and 1990s a new wave of Jews arrived from Russia.

The immigrants were very entrepreneurial. They developed retail stores all over downtown and the north side (with two early exceptions on the south side). In the early years, Broadway was one of the thriving streets for Jewish businesses. Immigrants also opened delis on Walnut Street, Vliet Street, North Avenue, Center Street, and Burleigh Street.

In 1924 the Jewish population developed their own Yiddish language newspaper, *Milwauker Wochenblat*. They also formed an extensive list of self-help agencies including (but not limited to) Jewish Family Services, the Jewish Community Center, United Jewish Appeal, and the Milwaukee Jewish Federation.

As time passed, the Jewish community became involved in the professions and organized healthcare facilities, schools, and law firms. Examples included Mount Sinai Hospital (today Aurora Sinai Medical Center), Hillel Academy, Yeshiva Elementary, and the law firms of Habush Habush & Rottier SC and Gimbel, Reilly, Geurin & Brown.

Notables

The Jewish community in the Milwaukee area produced many notables. A limited list is provided below.

Golda Meir (nee Mabovitch) was a Ukrainian-born Jew whose family ran a grocery store on the Milwaukee's near north side. Meir became involved in Zionist activism and later served as Israel's Minister of Labor, Foreign Minister, and became the **Prime Minister in** 1969. She was Israel's first woman prime minister and the world's fourth woman ever to hold such an office.

A Jewish Museum of Milwaukee docent learning about Milwaukee's connections to Golda Meir and the State of Israel in the Museum's permanent exhibit (photo courtesy of Jewish Museum of Milwaukee)

Victor Berger was a founding member of the Social Democratic Party of America and the first Socialist to be elected to the United States House of Representatives from Milwaukee.

Herbert Kohl ran a family-owned grocery chain (Kohl's) and was elected to the United States Senate between 1989 and 2013. He was also an owner of the Milwaukee Bucks of the National Basketball Association.

Allan H. (Bud) Selig purchased the major league Seattle Pilots in 1970 and moved the team to Milwaukee, renaming it the Milwaukee Brewers. He was the team's principle owner until 1998 and later became the ninth Commissioner of Baseball.

Rabbi Jacob Twerski was descended from notable rabbis in Eastern Europe. He founded Congregation Beth Jehudah and was succeeded by his son Michael and grandson Benzion.

Florence Eiseman was a nationally recognized clothing designer who opened a children's clothing business in Milwaukee in 1945.

Ben Marcus founded the Marcus Foundation, which included restaurants (such as the local Big Boy franchise), hotels, movie theaters and resorts in the Milwaukee area.

Harry Soref invented the laminated steel padlock and founded the Master Lock Company, the world's largest padlock manufacturer.

Sherman Park area

The Sherman Park neighborhood on Milwaukee's northwest side was historically home to many members of the Jewish population. The Sherman Park area began developing in the late teens and early twenties of the twentieth century. Milwaukeeans generally were attracted to the suburban look of the blocks with their wide, tree-lined streets and boulevards. But the beautiful homes were the neighborhood's signature. The large bungalows, duplexes, and Period Revival homes were finely crafted from brick, wood, and stone. Many Jewish families began joining Czechs and Germans who were moving to the area. Soon the Jewish population was 10,000 strong in Sherman Park and kosher markets and Jewish delis became part of the landscape. Some of the Jewish notables mentioned in the above section were raised in the neighborhood, including Herb Kohl and Bud Selig.

However, as the Jewish population became more prosperous they began leaving Sherman Park for Milwaukee's northern suburbs such as Glendale, River Hills, Fox Point, and Mequon. For nearly twenty years the Jewish presence in Sherman Park nearly disappeared. But this all changed in the 1990s when a new community of Jews began migrating to the area.

The original Jewish population in Sherman Park had been a mix of Orthodox, Reform, Conservative, and non-practicing Jews. The new arrivals were Chasidic Jews seeking an affordable community near a synagogue. The synagogue they sought was Beth Jehudah at 3100 North Fifty-Second Street where the notable Twerskis (see above) served as rabbis.

The new Jewish community in Sherman Park has continued to grow and is now over 200 families strong. In addition to the synagogue, they have developed their own self-help organizations and a school, Yeshiva Elementary School (YES).

Where to observe Jewish culture

A wonderful place to learn more about the Jewish presence in Milwaukee is to visit the Jewish Museum of Milwaukee. This museum is dedicated to preserving and presenting the Jewish history in southeastern Wisconsin and celebrating the continuum of Jewish heritage and culture.

The museum has permanent and rotating exhibits ranging from the history of the local Jewish community to Jews in fashion, sports, and popular culture.

The Jewish Museum of Milwaukee can be accessed at 1360 North Prospect Avenue most weekdays and Sundays. To learn more about the museum, visit their website at http://www.jewishmuseummilwaukee.org/index.php.

Window scrims and timeline in the Museum's permanent exhibit addressing significant historical and cultural events and figures (photo courtesy of Jewish Museum of Milwaukee)

Holidays and Traditions display in the Museum's permanent exhibit (photo courtesy of Jewish Museum of Milwaukee)

The Hmong

The Hmong began immigrating to America and Milwaukee in the late 1970s. This was made possible in 1975 when Congress approved the immigration of some Hmong to the United States under the "parole" power of the U.S. Attorney General.

Why did this happen? Let's start at the beginning. Hmong recorded history goes back to at least 2,000 BC in China. In the early nineteenth century, some Hmong began to migrate southward into the mountainous regions of Thailand, northern Burma, Vietnam, and Laos. Some of those who settled in Laos would end up in the United States. Many Lao Hmong had been aligned with the United States' military efforts during the Vietnam War. When the war ended, Laos gradually fell to the Communists, and the Hmong faced genocide. Thousands of Hmong fled Laos for refugee camps in Thailand. The United States Congress intervened and approved the immigration of those Hmong families that had supported the US war efforts.

Immigrants

Hmong arrived in America in their greatest numbers in the late 1970s through the 1990s. Following a period of secondary migration within the United States, substantial numbers of Hmong ended up in Wisconsin, making them the largest Asian group in the state.

But immigration to the United States was not easy. The Hmong who had lost so many lives in Laos, and whose cultural and life practices had been wrenched from them by the war and the camps, now faced radically new challenges. In the mountains of Southeast Asia the Hmong were subsistence farmers. As low-tech horticulturalists, Hmong households produced most of their basic necessities, and rarely had access to anything else. In post-industrial United States, most workers sold their labor and purchased their basic necessities plus much, much more. Very few of the complex life skills the Hmong had acquired in their mountain homes were relevant for this new world.

In their mountain homelands, Hmong artisans and craftspeople commanded high status. Hmong art forms are praised for their intricacy, symbolic expression, and beauty. They now entered a world where artistry drew *some* respect, but the greatest status and economic resources tended to go to those with formal educations and skills in advanced technology. In Southeast Asia, the Hmong had little access to education. Until very recently, they did not even have a written language.

Every facet of daily living in urban America involved new learning experiences. The Hmong had to learn everything from use of electricity and indoor plumbing to driving a car to banking to operating computers.

In addition, social organization among the Hmong was based on large extended families, lineages, and highly complex clan systems. In the United States, families were relatively small and few groups were organized along lineage or extended family lines. The U.S. economic system—with the emphasis on mobility and the selling of labor—tended to *disperse* rather than unify family groups.

And yet, against all odds, the Hmong in the United States and in Milwaukee, succeeded. In less than thirty years, the Hmong were becoming well integrated into the U.S. economy and social fabric, while retaining most of their traditions. Some were able to retain their healthy eating habits through gardening and participating in farmers' markets throughout the city.

In Milwaukee, the Hmong have their own newspapers, educational organizations, women's associations, arts and crafts clubs, a small museum, food markets, youth programs, family services, and student associations. And through education, the Hmong have advanced socially and economically in nearly every field they have entered.

"In Laos, meat was costly. Growing vegetables was more widely available. Hmong had no high blood pressure, cholesterol, diabetes. This is new here. A lot of exercising [in Laos], working on farm, hot weather. Coming here is different. Less activities, lots of meat here. Vegetables often cost more than meat. Produce not natural anymore. See more gout even today."

Quote of Hmong informant from the 12-year ethnic study conducted by Urban Anthropology Inc

Where to observe Hmong culture

One of the best venues to learn about Hmong traditional (and contemporary) life is at a local Hmong New Year's celebration. At these events, Hmong dress in traditional clothing and enjoy traditional foods, dance, music, and other forms of entertainment. Thousands attend from Milwaukee County and other areas. They are usually held in December at the State Fair Grounds in West Allis or the Franklin Sports Complex in Franklin.

    To get exact dates and locations, contact them at www.facebook.com/Hmong.Milwaukee.NewYear.

Chapter Three: Special populations

Chapter Three includes information on special ethnic groups with populations in Milwaukee County under 10,000. By "special" the authors mean that the groups (a) made significant contributions to the history of Milwaukee County, (b) are currently on the rise in the area, or (c) had engaging experiences in Milwaukee County.

Those included in this chapter (in alphabetical order) are the Burmese, Czechs/Slovaks, Greeks, Kashubes, North American Indians, Puerto Ricans, and Scots. As in the other chapters, the groups will be presented historically. Those with large population waves arriving earlier will be presented first and those with large population waves arriving later will be presented last.

The North American Indians

American Indians in Milwaukee County are a diverse group. Today the largest number of local Indians come from the Ojibwe, Oneida, Ho-Chunk, Potawatomi, and Stockbridge-Munsee nations.

Milwaukee migrations

Some local American Indians migrate back and forth between Milwaukee County and the reservations or settlements of their own nations, while others live exclusively in the Milwaukee area. Most of these nations were also those that had settled in Southeastern Wisconsin (and the area that would later be known as Milwaukee) before the Europeans arrived. But several hundred years of European encroachment on the land and treaties broken by the American government resulted in the removal of these nations to reserved parcels of land far away from the Milwaukee area.

What brought them back? To answer that question, let's look at the combined push/pull factors that the indigenous Wisconsin population faced. As Milwaukee developed into a European-style city, some native people routinely traveled to Milwaukee for trading and employment opportunities. At times, Milwaukee officials invited Indians back to participate in ceremonies such as the opening of Lincoln Memorial Drive and Bridge in 1929, or for the construction of lakefront villages in partnership with the Milwaukee Public Museum in the 1930s.

Wisconsin Indian exhibit at Milwaukee Public Museum

But the United States government, that had initially maneuvered the Wisconsin Indians onto reservations, gradually reversed its policies. Some agencies began to express written concerns that the native population had not assimilated into the wider US society. The goals then became the disintegration of these settlement communities, or, as some flatly stated—the "de-Indianizing" of the indigenous people.

One implemented policy was the boarding school, where between 1870 and well into the twentieth century, Indian children were taken from their families and taught the customs of white settlers. Some Wisconsin Indians began to leave the reservations to avoid personal and cultural loss of their children.

In the middle of the twentieth century, the US government instituted new policies—again designed to de-Indianize the native population. One policy, called the Voluntary Relocation Program, was designed to move Indians off the reservation into cities.

However, when the native people arrived in Milwaukee from the rural settlements, few had the needed skills or support systems to thrive in an urban environment. Furthermore, the urban migrants often lost access to the educational, health, and social service benefits they had negotiated on the reservations. Most of these government-sponsored benefits were restricted to those on reservations and then only to native people with a certain blood quantum of that nation. Many of the urban Indians no longer held residency on their reservations and many also had intermarried with non-Indians or with members of other Indian nations and could not meet the blood quantum requirement.

> "Pan Indian culture developed because of relocation in urban centers. Some are third, fourth, fifth generations off the reservation. In the city you're identified more as Indian than your tribal affiliation. It's actually more traditional in some respects. You have to maintain your heritage because it's not recognized or reinforced by the larger society. On the reservation you have the language, family, and common history."
>
> *Quote of North American Indian informant from the 12-year ethnic study conducted by Urban Anthropology Inc*

Urban Indian culture

It would be at this point in history that Indians in the city began to tighten their networks. An Urban Indian culture was emerging in Milwaukee. The urban Indians built successful businesses. They contributed professionals to domains such as education, healthcare, the legal system, and human services, and developed programs to serve the wider community. In addition, successfully-run efforts such as the Potawatomi casino contributed a vast inventory of resources to the wider community—both in terms of employment opportunities and in terms of direct grants to non-profit organizations.

The efforts at de-Indianizing Wisconsin's indigenous people had failed. If anything, cultural practices among Wisconsin's Indian nations increased over the years. Much of this revival has occurred in the City of Milwaukee and its surrounding suburbs. Native people in Milwaukee today demonstrate their commitment to Indian life ways in all aspects of daily living. Practices range from language preservation, to sweat lodges, to music, to dancing, to dress, to Indian gaming, to naming ceremonies, to an Indian Community School, to food, to powwows, to traditional vocations.

Where to observe urban Indian culture

A wonderful place to experience Milwaukee's Urban Indian culture is at Indian Summer at the Henry J. Maier Festival Park on Lake Michigan's shores. Here you can meet indigenous people from a variety of tribes, participate in a traditional powwow, visit tribal villages, watch American Indian traditional and contemporary entertainers, observe cultural demonstrations, listen to storytellers, and watch Lacrosse demos and tournaments. In addition, you can try traditional foods such as fry bread and buffalo meat and shop at the Native farmers market or craft marketplace.

Indian Summer is held annually in September. For information on specific events and times, contact www.indiansummer

The Scots/Scots Irish

Scots, often from the Scottish Highlands, began settling in the United States as traders and planters in the late 1600s. They were deeply involved in the tobacco trade in Virginia. A few joined the English and French and came to Wisconsin as fur traders during the same period.

The Scots Irish were Scottish Lowlanders who were promised land and work in Ireland under the British Ulster Plantation System in the early 1600s. When this system began failing in the early 1700s, these Ulster Scots began a long series of migrations to North America. The first wave of Ulster Scots (now known as the Scots Irish) came to Massachusetts in 1718. They soon migrated into Pennsylvania and other states throughout Appalachia, settling much of the south. As they moved, they changed the American landscape by introducing the settlement pattern of the isolated homestead surrounded by farmlands, as opposed to the earlier pattern of houses clustered in villages surrounded by the farmlands. Both the Scottish Highlanders and Lowlanders usually practiced the Presbyterian faith.

When the Revolutionary War broke out, most of the Scots Irish supported the American cause. This was not true of the Scottish highlanders who had strong commercial ties to the British Isles. The Highland community of Cape Fear valley and upstate New York were strong centers of Loyalist resistance. Of note, Scottish Loyalists were defeated by Scots Irish Patriots in the Battle of Kings Mountain in 1780. When the Americans won the war, many Scottish Loyalists emigrated to Canada.

After the war, most Scots who arrived in Wisconsin migrated from Canada; most Scots Irish who arrived in Wisconsin migrated from the American South.

Local notables

One Scottish immigrant who did not follow the above migration pattern was Alexander Mitchell. He was born in Ellon, Aberdeenshire, Scotland, and immigrated to the United States and Wisconsin in 1839. He developed a strong career in banking in Milwaukee. He also founded the Marine Bank of Wisconsin; served as president of the Chicago, Milwaukee and St.,

Paul Railway between 1864 and 1887; and was a US senator and a judge.

Mitchell built an abode on Grand Avenue (now Wisconsin Avenue) that stands today as the Wisconsin Club. It began as a modest brick house between Ninth and Tenth Streets in 1848. Mitchell then began buying up adjacent properties and expanded the house into an Italianate-style mansion.

Alexander Mitchell's son, John Mitchell, was a strong contributor to Milwaukee. A Civil War veteran, John Mitchell also served as a senator in the Wisconsin State Legislature and as a representative and senator in the United States' Congress.

Alexander Mitchell's grandson, Billy Mitchell, served as brigadier general in the U.S. Army Air Service. After World War One, Billy Mitchell began strongly advocating for increased investment in military air power. In 1925 he was court-martialed for insubordination after accusing Army and Navy leaders of an "almost unreasonable administration of the national defense" for investing in battleships instead of aircraft carriers. After his death, many military experts began heeding Mitchell's advice. Today he is credited by many as being the father of the United States Air Force. Milwaukee's main airport, General Mitchell International Airport, is named after him.

Scottish culture

Banking, venture capitalism, and military prowess were skills many other Scots brought with them to Wisconsin. In addition, some Scots were recruited from their homeland as artisans. Local companies such as ATI Ladish Company in Cudahy and the Falk Corporation in the City of Milwaukee recruited and employed a large number of people of Scottish heritage.

Scots and Scots Irish have also made cultural contributions. Two organizations in the Milwaukee area support Scottish culture. The first, St. Andrew's Society of the City of Milwaukee, was established by Alexander Mitchell in 1859 and exists today. The Society's mission is "to unite local Scots for benevolent purposes and to provide a framework for social and cultural activities." Another is the Robert Burns Club of Milwaukee, which is dedicated to preserving the living memory of Scotland's great, eighteenth century poet and lyricist, Robert Burns. Both organizations hold dinners and meetings in honor of the great bard.

These organizations were also instrumental in advocating for a small park in honor of Robert Burns. The Burns Commons Park, with a statue of Burns, can be visited at the corner of East Knapp Street and North Farwell Avenue.

"The Scots in Milwaukee have been getting together since the 1840s when there was a potato famine in Ireland and Scotland, and the Scots in Milwaukee got together to raise funds for the relief of the people in Scotland. And they decided at the time that they would hold a banquet honoring Robert Burns the poet of Scotland, the bard, and they began that tradition of banquets which has continued to this day. We are very proud of the fact that it is the longest continuously running social or ethnic event in the history of the state of Wisconsin."

Quote of Scottish informant from the 12-year ethnic study conducted by Urban Anthropology Inc

Where to observe Scottish culture

The most robust place to observe Scottish culture today is at the Highland Games. Each year the local Scots and Scots Irish organize the Milwaukee Highland Games/Scottish Fest (usually held in Wauwatosa) and the Wisconsin Highland Games (usually held in Waukesha). Events include live music, a parade of Tartans, highland dancing, piping, sheepdog demonstrations, haggis taco-eating contests, *Ceilidh* live music, horse exhibitions, and axe throwing competitions.

For information on exact dates, times, and venues, go to Wisconsin Highland Games at http://www.wisconsinscottish.org/info or Milwaukee Highland Games/Scottish Fest at http://milwaukeescottishfest.com/.

The Czechs/Slovaks

Czechs and Slovaks are often grouped together because they both once inhabited the nation of Czechoslovakia. However, today Czechs are people living in the Czech Republic (an area that was once part of the Austrian Empire) and Slovaks are people living in Slovakia (an area that was once part of the Kingdom of Hungary).

Immigrants

Czechs were in Milwaukee very early. Vojta Naprstek, a Czech patriot, came to Milwaukee in 1848—the year Wisconsin became a state. He found a number of Czechs already living in the city. Six years after his arrival, the Czechs/Slovaks founded an ethnic organization, *Slovanska Lipa*.

In the latter half of the nineteenth century and the first half of the twentieth century, most Czechs and Slovaks lived on Milwaukee's near south side. Today many live in Milwaukee County's southern suburbs, including Franklin and Cudahy.

Czech/Slovak culture

In 1868, T.J. Sokol Gymnastics Association was founded. Two years later the gymnastics club and Slovanska Lipa united under one title—Sokol. The organization still exists today under the name of Sokol Milwaukee, and sponsors a newsletter, ethnic movie Sundays, scholarships, traditional dinners, picnics, a dance group, and gymnastic events.

Where to observe Czech/Slovak culture

A great way to experience Czech/Slovak culture is to attend one of Sokol's annual gymnastics exhibitions. Here youth gymnasts demonstrate their physical fitness skills and compete for metals. Opening and closing ceremonies include ethnic anthems.

For dates and venues of exhibitions go to www.sokol-milwaukee.org.

The Kashubes

The Milwaukee Kashubes built an urban fishing village on Jones Island in the late 1800s. You might ask: What is Jones Island and who were the Kashubes?

Jones Island is actually a peninsula that extends off the Milwaukee coast onto Lake Michigan. It was originally named after Captain James Monroe Jones, who owned a shipbuilding business there in the 1850s. The Kashubes were from the Baltic seacoast in Poland but had usually considered themselves separate from the Poles. Most of them were farmers and fisher folk, and they had their own distinct language and customs.

Immigrants

But in the 1870s the Kashubes faced some of the same challenges that the Poles faced. Prussian leader Otto Von Bismarck forced changes on them, limiting their use of their own language and the influence of the Catholic religion. As a result, many of them started coming to the United States and to Milwaukee.

In Milwaukee the Kashubes found Jones Island to be an almost ideal location. On the peninsula they were able to make a living as fisher folks and keep their basic lifestyle and traditions in the midst of a growing city. Instead of official representatives, the fishing village had informal leaders that spoke for the island population and advocated for its needs. A strong sense of community and cooperation made it possible for the Kashubes to survive independently.

Within the Milwaukee community they often faced "otherness." Poles looked down on them and considered them primitive. The local artist community romanticized the picturesque fishing village and traveled there to capture what seemed to be a survival from another era. Some Milwaukee-ans only knew Jones Island as a place for wild tavern parties and fish fries.

However, the peninsula was a desirable location for others as well. In the early twentieth century the city of Milwaukee decided they needed to build a sewage plant on Jones Island. One by one, the islanders were evicted. In 1944 tavern keeper Felix Struck was the last Kashube to leave the island. The fishing village was entirely gone. Most Kashubes moved to Bay View, the near south side, or southern suburbs.

> "Today there're people wanting to find out all about us, now that we've assimilated so much. Even some of the Poles accept us—some not so much."
>
> *Quote of Kashubian informant from the 12-year ethnic study conducted by Urban Anthropology Inc*

Where to observe Kashubian culture

In 1974 tiny Kaszub's Park was constructed as a memorial to the people that had once inhabited Jones Island. While it just might be the smallest park in the country, you will rarely find a Kashube who is not thrilled with it.

Currently, every first Saturday in August the Kashubes return for an annual picnic to celebrate their heritage. The picnic is open to outsiders. This is a wonderful place to observe what is left of Milwaukee Kashubian culture. Just access a good map and show up around noon at the park. On your way you'll see no remnants of the fishing village. You'll pass a sewage treatment plant, harbor facilities, silos full of grain, mountains of coal and road salt, and huge containers being stored on the peninsula. But you will experience the windswept atmosphere and sense of eerie seclusion that the Kashubes must have known on the island.

Find the park and be startled by its miniscule size. Enjoy the picnic. Talk to the Kashubes. They are just about the most friendly and fun-loving people you'll ever meet.

The Greeks

Greeks began arriving in Milwaukee County in small numbers at the turn of the twentieth century. Many came from the Peloponessus region, especially from Arcadia and to a much lesser extent from Sparta, Messenia, and Elias. Many found work in Milwaukee tanneries and others became confectioners, restaurateurs, coffeehouse owners, small grocers, barbers, and saloonkeepers.

Immigrants

The Greek immigrants and their businesses shaped several Milwaukee neighborhoods—neighborhoods that remained strongly Greek until the 1940s. These included the general areas of Fifth and Wells Streets, North Water Street and East Juneau Avenue, and Sixth Street and National Avenue. In the small colonies, Greek families would meet at coffee shops with compatriots of the same village in Greece to talk, exchange gossip, share religious and political ideologies, and play cards or games. New immigrants would seek out the coffee shops upon arriving in Milwaukee.

While it is not known when or by whom the first Greek restaurant was opened, the early Greek eateries were designed for the immigrant population. As time went on, some proprietors retained their Greek family or historic names such as Panhellenion, Acropolis, and Kentron, but more of them adopted Anglicized names such as the American Restaurant, Busy Bee Lunch, City Hall Lunch, and Sanitary Lunch. Today, Greek-run restaurants are all over Milwaukee County—some brandishing Greek names but most not.

Many members of the central city Greek population of the past have migrated to the suburb of Wauwatosa. This is also close to the two major Greek Orthodox churches—the Annunciation Greek Orthodox Church and Saints Constantine & Helen Greek Orthodox Church. The Annunciation Greek Orthodox Church was designed by architect Frank Lloyd Wright in 1956 as one of Wright's last works. Opened in 1962 after his death, the church design was intended to reflect traditional Byzantine architectural forms, reinterpreted for a modern context.

Where to observe Greek culture

Both churches hold annual festivals to share Greek culture. Excellent places to enjoy Greek bands, Hellenic dancers, cultural demonstrations, and Greek dishes such as such as *koulouria, skishkebobs, gyros, baklava,* or *Yiayia's spanakopita* are at Greek Fest sponsored by the Annunciation Greek Orthodox Church and held at the State Fair Park (640 South Eighty-Fourth Street in West Allis) or Grecian Fest held at Saints Constantine & Helen Greek Orthodox Church (2160 North Wauwatosa Avenue). Both festivals are usually convened in June. For more information on dates, locations, entertainment, and activities, contact https://www.facebook.com/MkeGreekFest or http://stsconstantinehelenwi.org/.

The Puerto Ricans

The first signs of Puerto Rican immigration to Milwaukee began in the 1940s. They were called *Primeros*. While most came from Puerto Rico, some were migrants from Michigan where they'd worked as migrant farmworkers. Factory jobs at that time in Milwaukee allowed many Puerto Ricans to leave migrant work for industrial jobs that would provide stability for their families. In 1951, Milwaukee foundries, in need or workers, recruited 100 Puerto Ricans.

The industrial needs were great. In 1960 the Puerto Rican population was 2820; by 1970 it was 5889.

The immigrants

The Puerto Rican arrivals mainly took root in two neighborhoods. A small group settled in the Third Ward just south of downtown, and a larger group settled in the Yankee Hill neighborhood just north of downtown. Upon arrival, people from the same villages and cities in Puerto Rico formed hometown clubs. They maintained many of their traditions, including house parties, the Feast of the Three Kings (*El Dia des Los Reyes*), and a special form of Christmas caroling called *parranda*.

Most of the settlers were Catholic (although some joined the Pentecostal movement). In the Yankee Hill neighborhood the Puerto Rican residents quickly made Old Saint Mary's Church—once a chief place of worship for German Catholics—their central community.

Like so many ethnic groups in Milwaukee, both the Third Ward and the Yankee Hill Puerto Rican communities were displaced by urban renewal and freeway building. Most later migrated into the Riverwest neighborhood and made their homes around the area of Holton and Locust Streets. There they still enjoyed playing dominoes on porches, celebrating Puerto Rican holidays, and jamming island music. Some also moved to the south side.

"People often think Mexicans in Milwaukee are just like Puerto Ricans. This is not the case at all. For one thing, you see most Mexicans on the south side and most Puerto Ricans on the north side. There are so many differences in food and music and dance and even family types, but also Mexicans tended to be Spaniards mixed with the indigenous population and Puerto Ricans were often Spaniards and other Europeans mixed with Africans. You see a lot of African customs in the Caribbean which were not picked up in Mexico, especially in the Catholic religion."

Quote of Puerto Rican informant from the 12-year ethnic study conducted by Urban Anthropology Inc

Notables

Although Puerto Ricans are a relatively small community in the Milwaukee area, they have no shortage of notables. Just a few will be listed below.

The parents of Perfecto Rivera had left a mountain village near Comerio, Puerto Rico for Milwaukee in 1953. As a teenager, Perfecto attended Pulaski High School. He was a very popular student and was nominated to the court of the junior prom. When teachers objected, the principal argued that Rivera did not appropriately represent the student body and he should disqualify himself. When Rivera did not, the students went ahead and elected him king. Years later, Rivera became a banking professional and public service manager. In 2006, he ran an unsuccessful campaign for the United States House of Representatives.

In the 1950s, Puerto Rican Felix Mantilla played baseball for the Milwaukee Braves. He met his wife in town and made Milwaukee his home. In his honor, a Little League Baseball federation was formed, called the Felix Mantilla League.

A Puerto Rican Olympian also had roots in Milwaukee. Boxer Israel "Shorty" Acosta left Puerto Rico to train at the gym of the United Community Center in the 1970s. Foiled in his opportunity to participate in the U.S Olympic team in 1980 because of the U.S. boycott over the Soviet Union's invasion of Afghanistan, he was able ultimately to participate at age 31 in the Los Angeles games.

John M. Torres became a pioneer writer and broadcaster in Milwaukee. In 1975 he became the first Latino writer for the *Milwaukee Journal's* Latin Corner column and later became the first Latino reporter for WISN-TV. He also served as editor for *La Guardia,* a Milwaukee bilingual newspaper.

Where to observe Puerto Rican culture

A good place to observe Puerto Rican culture is at Puerto Rican Fest, which began under the Thirty-Fifth Street viaduct on Milwaukee's south side in 2013 and moved to Humboldt Park in Bay View in 2015. The festival, which is held in mid-summer, has been sponsored by local *El Conquistador* Newspaper, Yussef Morales, and the Puerto Rican Empowerment Group of Wisconsin.

At Puerto Rican Fest, you can experience Puerto Rican bands, a car show, motorcycle exhibits, and traditional Puerto Rican food—including roasted pig. For information on times and places, check with the *El Conquistador* website at http://www.conquistadornews.com/. But arrive early if you want to eat, as vendors have run out of food early due to unexpectedly large crowds.

The Burmese

Due to internal unrest in Burma (the Republic of Myanmar), Burmese populations have arrived in the United States in three waves—one in the 1960s, one following an uprising in 1988, and one after 2006. Between 2006 and 2015, more than 60,000 Burmese were resettled in the United States. This was mainly due to ethnic conflicts and a series of economic and political protests and demonstrations that took place in 2007. A few Burmese also resettled following the devastating effects of Hurricane Nargis in 2008 that resulted in an estimated 200,000 people dead or missing. Survivors of these events went to refugee camps in Malaysia or along Indian, Bangladeshi, and Thai borders. Some were allowed entry to the United States.

Most of the Milwaukee Burmese have arrived in this last wave. As of 2015 there were an estimated 1,500 Burmese people living in the greater Milwaukee area.

The immigrants

Most of the Burmese who arrived in the United States were refugees. Under US law, refugees and asylees are aliens who are unable or unwilling to return to their country of origin or nationality because of persecution or well-founded fears of persecution. Much of the persecution the Burmese refugees experienced in Burma was prompted by their ethnic and religious affiliations. While there are at least 108 different ethnolinguistic groups in Burma, the Bamar (also called Burman) ethnic group comprises over two-thirds of the national population and has dominated the political and cultural environ-

117

ment since the British left the country in 1948—a process often described by insiders and outsiders as the "Burmanization" of Burma. Ethnic persecution, including killings, rape, and forced labor, has been well-documented.

In addition to ethnic discrimination, there has also been religious discrimination in Burma. Between 85 and 89 percent of the population of Burma practices Buddhism, mostly Theravada Buddhism. Seven percent of the population practices Christianity, 4 percent Islam, 2 percent Hinduism, and approximately 2 percent other faiths. Muslims and Christians have experienced persecution because of their religions.

Some of the worst examples of human rights abuses have occurred among the Muslim Burmese—particularly the Rohingya people. Many Muslim Burmese spent decades moving back and forth between Burma and Malaysia. The Burmese regime has refused to acknowledge them as citizens. As of 2015, more than 100,000 Rohingyas of Burma live in camps for internally displaced persons. Many of these have made their way to America and to the Milwaukee area. Many who had settled in Malaysia have also resettled in America and the Milwaukee area.

Also included among the Milwaukee Burmese population are members of the Karen ethnic group, who practice Christianity or Buddhism, and the Chin ethnic group, whose members are mainly Christians. Other smaller groups in Milwaukee include Karenni, Shan, and Burman/Bamar populations—most who practice Theravada Buddhism, Christianity, or traditional local religions.

Keeping the culture in Milwaukee

Like the Milwaukee Hmong, the Burmese want to adapt to American norms but not lose their own cultural traditions. Currently, many refugees are being assisted in adaptation to America by the International Learning Center, the Burmese Immigration Project, Pan-African Community Association, the International Institute of Wisconsin, International Language

Center and Tutoring, Lutheran Social Services, Catholic Charities, Neighborhood House, coalitions of landlords, and Ascension Lutheran Church. Many refugees have been able to remain in their extended family groups by renting apartments in the same complex—some of these, such as the Rohingya /Burmese Muslims and Chin are on Milwaukee's south side. The Karen refugees have tended to settle on the north side near Washington Park.

The refugees have retained most of their Burmese diets and food restrictions, made possible in part by opening Burmese stores in Milwaukee. Most Burmese prefer rice and spicy curry dishes with vegetables and meats.

They have also organized faith communities to help them retain their culture and meet their spiritual needs. The Chin and Kachin have their own churches, and the Buddhists and Muslims have their own temple and mosque.

The Burmese people have also retained their interpersonal customs. They are especially polite and show vigilant respect for elders and mentors. To acknowledge this deference, they use different linguistic terms for men and women by age relative to their own age.

The Burmese have developed practices in Milwaukee to remember their persecution in Burma. One of these practices, observed by a few, is memorializing the "8888 uprising" which occurred August 8, 1988. On that day in 1988, peaceful demonstrations for democracy began spreading across the country, ending with a military coup and the slaughter of thousands of protesters by the military-led government and thousands more fleeing to refugee camps. In Milwaukee, some Burmese still honor this event on its anniversary. On the day, they gather together, pray for those who lost their lives in the uprising, and talk about a dream of a Burma free from military rule.

Other observances include Mon National Day and Chin National Day. The Karen practice an annual spiritual day with a bracelet-tying ceremony. A water/new year ceremony also draws a large number of people in April. The Rohingya and Burmese Muslims observe Muslim holidays.

"You don't date people openly, and since you don't really date people outside of your own culture, then you don't see them often enough to get to know them. You don't move out until you get married. . . . I think that here in Milwaukee you Americans would go out on weekend days and people would go out to bars, but our culture—it's not open or maybe there are language barriers that make this hard, and stop us from going out and being more social with others. The Burmese refuges [Chin, Karen] would say that since the community is very small, and if a girl would go out a lot on her own, this is not looked good on or respected as much."

Quote of Burmese informant from the 12-year ethnic study conducted by Urban Anthropology Inc

---

Where to observe Burmese culture

World Refugee Day is a good place to observe Burmese culture. The Day was established by the United Nations to honor the courage, strength, and determination of those who have been forced to flee their homes under threat of conflict.

In Milwaukee County, the day is usually held in June at one or more local parks. The Burmese are strong participants, as are Hmong, East Africans, Eastern Europeans, Latin Americans, and other cultural groups. People usually bring their own picnic lunches while they watch or participate in cultural performances and games, such as soccer. You will see people outfitted in their traditional dress, practicing their indigenous customs, and eating traditional foods.

To learn more about World Refugee Day in Milwaukee County, including times and places, consult the website: https://www.facebook.com/MilwaukeeWorldRefugeeDay.

Made in the USA
Middletown, DE
26 November 2022

15849488R00069